THE BIG BOOK OF
GLEEB

THE BIG BOOK OF GLEEB

PAUL B. LOWNEY

Illustrations by Frank Renlie

DODD, MEAD & COMPANY
New York

FOREWORD
By Steve Allen

The fact that one writes a foreword to a book obviously establishes that one recommends it to the reader. In this case I recommend it to readers two at a time. Since "The Big Book of Gleeb" is mostly written in the form of dialogue, I suggest that you sit down in a chair large enough to accommodate your husband, wife, sweetheart, fiancé, son, daughter, grandchild — or whatever turns you on — and start reading aloud.

Many of Paul Lowney's "gleebisms" are fun for fun's sake; others are funny on the outside but have a moral center. I don't know exactly how properly to describe this imaginative type of prose; anyway, I'd rather read it than describe it. I only wish I'd thought of it first.

"The Big Book of Gleeb" will appeal mostly to a certain type of reader. The trick is to find out if you're that type. I can assure you that finding out is a heady experience. It's the sort of book which will be found in Christmas stockings, on coffee tables, and in the hands of bright people everywhere. I suspect that it will be as fresh a century from now as it is today.

Mr. Lowney has not forgotten that adults, as well as children, can delight in sheer nonsense, so he uses it generously throughout his book. But some apparent nonsense has meaning behind it, if you look closely. What makes "The Big Book of Gleeb" fascinating is the variety of areas it touches upon — humor, love, philosophy, science, psychology, ethics.

"The Big Book of Gleeb" is basically humorous, but it conveys more than humor. Many of its passages reflect the probings of an inquiring mind sensitive to the human condition and the incongruities and contradictions in our everyday existence. It will evoke warmth and tenderness, yet in another instance it will cut as sharply and devastatingly as Cyrano's rapier.

Most of all, "The Big Book of Gleeb" is fun. While at times it lays bare some of life's more serious and painful aspects, it leaves one with a good feeling. Any book that can do that is worth having around.

Someone filled our swimming pool with
live piranha.
If we don't swim there anymore,
The piranha will starve.

I found an ocean of gleeb.
What will you do with it?
Paint the world.
All of it?
No, just the inside.
Why not the outside?
Would you care to live in a world full
of "Wet Gleeb" signs?

Say something wise.
"Love someone."
Say something wiser.
"Love yourself."

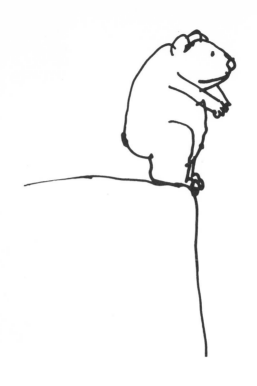

I'm going to move to the forest and live off nature with my bare hands.

What will you eat?

Plants and animals.

How will you kill the animals?

I don't believe in killing animals.

What will you do?

I'll teach them to commit suicide.

What are you doing?

Writing a letter to my psychiatrist.

What for?

I'm telling him I no longer need treatment because I am now emotionally mature, well-adjusted, and secure.

What if he disagrees with you?

I'll break his glasses.

I can't marry you.

Why not?

You're too old for me.

You can subtract part of my age.

How is that possible?

I was sick for three years.

Be serious.

There's another way we can look at it.

How?

I plan to live to 105, which will make you eighty-seven, and if you think I'll be too old for an eighty-seven-year-old woman, you are mistaken.

Be practical.

I have another solution.

What is it?

I can equalize our ages.

How?

Marry me and you'll age fast.

Are you opposed to a platonic relation-ship?

No.

Can we have one?

Certainly, as long as it's physical.

Why don't you take her out?
She always says she's busy.
Doing what?
Things she wants to do.
What makes her say she's always busy?
Things she doesn't want to do.

Ever been arrested?
Yes — last April.
What for?
Selling elixir of youth to aging matrons.
Any other arrests?
One.
What for?
Same offense.
When?
Summer of 1805.

Do you believe in astrology?
No.
Why not?
We Virgos are born skeptics.

How can you and I find truth?

Through precise investigation.

But some truths don't lend themselves to precise investigation.

In those cases, we'll use rational logic.

That presents a problem.

What problem?

Whose rational logic shall we use — yours or mine?

A dandelion farmer
Found tulips growing in his field.
He pulled them up and said,
"Weeds are such a nuisance."

Being in the minority
Is so popular nowadays,
There are very few left
In the majority.

Why are you so active in animal welfare work?

Because of my man-animal philosophy.

Explain your philosophy.

Man's superiority on Earth does not grant him moral or ethical license to inflict suffering upon animals — and especially not for unnecessary or frivolous things such as rodeos, bullfights, zoos, dog races, cockfights, fox hunting, steel trapping, game and trophy hunting, and senseless laboratory experiments.

What are you trying to achieve in this area?

A reduction in suffering for all forms of animal life.

That certainly is an unselfish dedication on your part.

It is not entirely unselfish.

Why not?

I believe in reincarnation.

When something annoys me,
I say that "something" doesn't exist.
And if it doesn't exist,
It can't annoy me.
But then something else annoys me —
My self-deception.

I get up, go to bed, get up, go to bed —
Day after day, after day, after day.
What's my natural state?
Am I asleep to get rested for waking?
Or am I awake to get tired for sleeping?

Are you having a nice lifetime?
Not particularly.
What are you doing about it?
I'm searching for a practical alternative.

Why are you standing on the corner?
I'm watching for my friend's blue car.
How long have you been standing here?
An hour.
Don't you think you ought to give up?
He'll be along soon.
What makes you think so?
Lately, a lot more blue cars have been coming by.

I'm depressed.

Cheer up; everything will turn out all right; keep a stiff upper lip; snap out of it.

I'm still depressed.

Every cloud has a silver lining; it's always darkest before the dawn; you'll feel better in the morning.

I'm still depressed.

Didn't my words help you any?

They sound all right, but they have absolutely no bearing on my problems.

Is it all right to lie?

Sometimes.

When?

When a lie is harmless and when the truth is harmful.

Is a harmless lie ever harmful?

Yes.

When?

When you get caught at it.

Want something to worry about?

No.

Everyone should have at least one good worry.

All right — what should I worry about?

The sun is going to expand 100 times its original size.

Really?

The heat will boil away our oceans.

Sounds grim.

The temperature will reach 4,000 degrees Fahrenheit and will melt rocks and leave this planet a lifeless inferno.

Is this fantasy?

No, scientific fact.

When will all this happen?

In five billion years.

Five billion years?

Yes.

Why should I worry about it now?

Must you wait until the last minute?

What's that odd-looking skeleton?
Paranthropus — an extinct hominid.
Is it male or female?
A male — named Albert.
And what's the small skeleton?
Albert as a child.

Sorry your marriage didn't work out.
There's still hope.
What makes you think so?
The divorce isn't working out either.

Let's run away together.
Why?
So we can live happily ever after.
Ever after?
Yes, possibly longer.

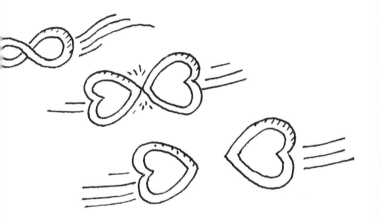

Say something to make me feel good.

Custard pie.

That's not what I had in mind.

Hot fudge sundae.

Try another approach.

You're lying on a beach of clean white sand washed by warm blue water, and you're caressed by blossom-scented tropical winds and delicious sunshine.

Can't you make it more personal?

I'm with you on that beach.

That's better.

What should I say now?

Something nice to complete the wonderful feeling of that scene.

You're having custard pie and I'm having a hot fudge sundae.

Why should I marry you?
Think what I can offer you.
What can you offer me?
Perfect happiness.
That's not enough.

Would you like to see the menu?

I've seen it already and it's very attractive.

Coffee?

Yes.

Cream?

Without cream, and if you are out of cream, I'll have it without milk.

Another cup of coffee?

No, coffee keeps me awake during the daytime.

Did you enjoy your dinner?

I'll let you know in two hours.

Why do you make such odd remarks?

I just can't stand the same old stereotyped chatter every day.

How did you like the new play?
I don't know.
Didn't you catch the opening last night?
I did.
Then why don't you know?
I haven't read the reviews.

Who was at the door?

A man dressed like Santa Claus.

What makes you think it wasn't Santa Claus?

This subpoena.

What's new?

I just heard on the radio that the moon mysteriously retarded its orbit and is spiraling toward Earth by force of gravity at a speed of 3,412 miles per hour, and will crash in about sixty-five hours, and the impact will explode the earth into a trillion pieces.

When did you hear this?

On the six o'clock news.

Did you happen to hear the score of the game?

That amoeba threatens to call the police.

Why?

He claims someone keeps peeping at him through a glass.

Nothing can kill the mad love I started
for you.

Nothing?

Well, maybe one thing.

What's that?

If you started a mad love for me.

If I'm too good to you, you'll like me
less.
Then don't be too good to me.
What should I be?
Be good to me.

Married or single?
Single.
Didn't you ever meet the right girl?
I did.
What happened?
She didn't meet the right fellow.

You are the world's leading graphologist?
Correct.
Do you analyze much handwriting?
I don't look at handwriting anymore.
Why not?
I'm retired.
What about the handwritten letters you get?
I ignore them.
Why?
The people who write them are irresponsible, crafty, egocentric and obsessed with materialism.

If I marry you, will you buy me jewels?
Yes.
Will you buy me a sports car?
Yes.
Will you buy me French perfumes?
Yes.
Will you buy me beautiful clothes?
Yes.
Will you fly me south in the winter?
Yes.
Will you wine me and dine me?
Yes.
I don't want to marry you.
Why not?
You squander money.

Aren't you supposed to be at your analyst's?

Yes.

Why aren't you?

I'm too depressed.

Can I lag behind?
What for?
I want to pick wild flowers.
What if you get lost?
What if I do?
Don't come running to me.

Infinity
Makes my brain numb.
It goes on and on and on
And on and on and on
And on and on and on ...
At this rate,
Where will it all end?

How many words are in the English language?

About 450,000.

Are there any of these words you have never seen or heard?

Thousands.

Name a few.

That man is risking his life without a net.

That's his business.

No, it's my business too.

Why?

If he falls, I'll get sick.

Of all the people
Who go window shopping,
Only an infinitesimal number
Ever buy windows.

Fifty-four per cent of the people
Said they believed
In angels.
Therefore,
Angels exist.

Friendship is a noble relationship.

Remember, "To have a friend, be a friend."

I have a friend,

But I'm sorry to say, my friend hasn't.

Everyone can claim his own star.

There are more than enough to go around.

A star is reliable
And good company
And just pointing to one
Won't wear it out.

I know when I'm talking out loud.
I can feel my lips moving
And I can hear words in my ears.
And if what I hear is interesting,
I shut up and listen.

Sometimes I can't stand living with myself.

I get on my nerves.

More than once I've threatened to move out.

Would you like to hear a poem I just wrote?

No.

Here it is:

"The sun is setting in the west.
It is the sun that I love best."

The answer is still "no."

What caused him to get so fat?
Whenever he was mad, he over-ate.
What made him mad?
People teased him about being skinny.

Make a mental note of that.
Okay.
I've changed my mind — tear it up.

Why do you boast so much?

Because of my rule.

What rule?

Never let modesty stand in the way of the facts.

I'm hungry.
But you ate a little while ago.
I did?
Yes, you had a sandwich.
I forgot about it.
Are you still hungry?
No.

He's unreasonable.

I disagree.

He's unrealistic.

I doubt it.

He's gauche.

Not really.

He's insensitive.

Wrong.

He's tasteless.

Unfounded.

He's pushy.

Stop!

Why?

These judgments are highly subjective and relative, yet you assign them as categorical truths.

They are truths.

How can you prove it?

By my dictum.

State your dictum.

"Truth is whatever I say it is."

Good afternoon — this is Mr. Brown's desk.

Are you a talking desk?

No, that's merely an expression.

Oh.

Can I help you?

Is Mr. Brown in?

Who's calling?

It's more polite to say, "May I ask who's calling?"

All right — may I ask who's calling?

You may ask.

Who's calling?

I won't tell you.

"Cogito ergo sum."
What does that mean?
"I think, therefore I exist."
Is this a true proposition?
An important philosopher thought so.
Then do me a favor.
Anything.
Stop thinking and vanish.

Do you live alone?

Yes.

Isn't it lonely?

There's a difference between "alone" and "lonely."

Explain the difference.

"Alone" is a state of being, "lonely" is a state of mind.

I know a psychological principle.

What is it?

If you are overly intent on wanting something to happen, chances are it won't.

I know the reverse of that principle. What is it?

If you are overly fearful that something will happen, chances are it will.

Life disturbs me.

Why?

It won't give me what I want.

You have two choices.

Name one.

Work on life so that it gives you what you want.

Name the other.

Work on your mind so that it believes that what life gives you is what you want.

The earth is getting warmer.

Why?

More and more people are generating more heat and the atmosphere is holding it in.

Is this bad?

Yes.

Why?

In time, the polar ice caps will melt.

What will that do?

It will raise our oceans two hundred feet and put thousands of cities underwater.

What can be done about this?

Scientists have a plan for refreezing the ice caps.

What's the plan?

When the ice caps start melting, they'll have all people on Earth open their refrigerator doors.

Have you heard of the theory of anti-matter?

Whether I say "yes" or "no," you're bound to tell me.

The theory is this: For every bit of matter, there is somewhere in the universe an equal and opposite bit of anti-matter.

Does this mean there could be anti-people?

According to the theory — yes.

Imagine, an anti-me.

Do you think you'd like anti-you?

I think we'd argue.

It is odd that people say,
"It's all in your head."
Certainly, it's in your head.
Everything in life is in your head.
It's not in your big toe.
If you stick a pin in your big toe,
The pain is registered in your head.
The next time someone says,
"It's all in your head,"
You say,
"Where do you think it is — in my big toe?"

A man I know keeps saying, "I'm no good in the morning until I've had my coffee."

I've seen him after he's had his coffee, and I can assure you, coffee has absolutely no effect on his goodness.

Philosophers say you really can't prove
the world of matter exists.

All you can prove is that our senses,
which sense matter, exist.

Well, I once took a look at the world,
And I have the sense to know that
something is the matter.

I'm always cold.

I can't understand why people call me cold-blooded.

If I were cold-blooded, the cold wouldn't bother me.

The warmth would.

In Arizona, signs all over the state read:
"See the Big Cactus Tree!"
People from miles around follow the signs.
They drive on narrow, bumpy roads, up mountains and through valleys.
They park their cars and hike a mile on a rocky pathway.
They find the big cactus tree,
And they walk around it and they look at it and they say:
"My, that's some big cactus tree!"

Climbing a mountain builds my pride.

I feel accomplishment in my triumph over nature.

The struggle against the mountain symbolizes my mortal combat with Fate.

When I conquer a mountain, I get the overwhelming feeling I own it.

That's probably why I try to bring it home with me.

If you want to know how to spell a word, you need two dictionaries.

One dictionary is for looking up the word.

The other is for spelling the word so you can look it up.

How do you know what is right and what is wrong?

I trust my conscience.

Is conscience an infallible source of ethical judgment?

It is, if you use it with absolute honesty.

Are you saying that there are as many standards of right and wrong as there are individual consciences?

Is that bad?

It's chaos.

Why?

Consciences can support widely divergent behavior — good, evil, social, antisocial, constructive, destructive — depending upon how they've been programed.

How would you set standards for right and wrong?

I'd say that, ultimately, right and wrong are what a body of reasonable people of goodwill decide they are.

And who decides what is "reasonable" and what is "goodwill?"

Reasonable people of goodwill.

I'm not particularly fond of introductions.

Why not?

I'm always meeting people I don't know.

That man is brilliant.

Actually he is not.

How do you know?

He just acts brilliant to cover up his stupidity.

Then he certainly is a good actor.

No, he is not that either.

Why not?

He's been acting brilliant for so long, he really believes it.

Want to hear some funny lines?

If you insist.

"A cat ate cheese and then waited for the mouse with baited breath."

Mmm.

"He couldn't swim the English Channel because he had so much grease on his body, he kept slipping out of the water."

Incredible.

"To sculpture an elephant, take a block of granite and chip away everything that doesn't look like an elephant."

Unbelievable.

"He was just a shell of his former self, and if you put him to your ear, you could hear the ocean."

Odd.

"I invented a universal solvent but now I can't find anything to keep it in."

All right.

"In certain sections of Tibet they cremate middle-aged schoolteachers at birth."

May I say a word?

Certainly.

Good-by.

Sometimes I feel like hiding.
What from?
People.
Do people want to find you?
No.
Then why hide?
I don't want to find them.

What's bothering you?
You.
Why?
You don't love me.
How do you know?
I know.
How?
By the way you act.
I haven't done anything.
That's how I know.

I don't know about Saturday night.
Why not?
I don't like to plan that far ahead.
Should I ask you again on Thursday?
By Thursday, I'll have a date.

Why were you so rude to him?

You heard his remark.

Last night a fellow made the same remark and you smiled.

That was different.

Why?

He was good-looking.

I can't go out with you anymore.
Why not?
You're too good for me.
What other faults do I have?

I can't seem to impress that girl.
You try too hard.
What's wrong with that?
People who try too hard generally fail.
What should I do.
Be yourself.
I'll fail at that, too.
Why?
I try too hard to be myself.

Your love protects me from everyone.
Everyone?
Yes.
You're forgetting one person.
Who?
Me.

Why did you suddenly start picking on her?

I just noticed her faults.

Why didn't you notice them before?

Before, I was in love.

Do you know what can make me happy?

What?

Friendship growing into love.

I know what can make you unhappy.

You're not going to say, "Love growing into friendship," are you?

What makes you think I'm not?

Why is she so upset?
She's unhappily in love.
She only thinks she's in love.
Are you certain?
Positive.
Then, I'll give her the good news.
What good news?
She only thinks she's upset.

What is your new boyfriend like?
He has a very special quality.
Is he handsome?
No.
Is he intellectual?
No.
Is he charismatic?
No.
Is he rich?
No.
What's his special quality?
He loves me.

Imagine, a cubic inch of matter weighing ten billion pounds.

Impossible.

Not for a pulsar.

What's a pulsar?

An enormously condensed, dying neutron star.

Has anyone ever seen one?

No.

How do you know it exists?

Scientists believe that the faint radio beeps arriving from outer space with an incredible regularity, unmatched by any known timepiece, are transmitted by small, rapidly spinning pulsars.

Is this fact or theory?

Theory.

Does the theory carry much weight?

Ten billion pounds per cubic inch.

Have you ever met anyone from outer space?

No.

What would they look like?

I don't know.

Then how do you know you've never met anyone?

Well, let's say I've never talked with anyone.

How can you be sure?

You just couldn't disguise an outer-space accent.

How can I live serenely?

Be inactive and don't get involved.

But that would bore me and make me restless.

Then be active and get involved.

But that would give me problems and make me nervous.

Why do you run so fast?
I'm trying to get away from myself.
Are you able to?
No, when I stop to rest, I catch myself.

Do you know what you want out of life?

Yes.

What?

Mutual affectionate response, status, peace of mind, good health, interesting new experiences, and satisfaction from worthwhile achievements.

Have you attained all this?

Yes.

How?

By having a happy, secure childhood.

What's the secret of that?

Having happy, secure parents.

Did you have such parents?

No.

Then how do you account for your success?

I had happy, secure baby-sitters.

Human love is good for plants.

Nonsense.

Human animosity is bad for plants.

Fiction.

Considerable evidence supports this theory.

For instance?

My dying cedar trees became healthy after I started talking to them.

You talk to trees?

It gets results.

The entire theory is too bizarre.

Then why do you practice it?

What makes you think I do?

I heard you swearing at weeds.

How do you measure infinity?

Simple — start at the end and measure to the beginning.

But infinity has no end.

Well, in that case, measure halfway from the beginning and multiply by two.

How did life on Earth start?

I can only guess.

Guess.

From a single living cell.

How did the cell start?

It would only be a guess.

Guess.

Cosmic rays bombarded a primitive sea containing methane and ammonia and finally, under exactly the right conditions, a cell was accidentally formed with the power to reproduce itself.

Is that the way it all happened?

I guess so.

Why don't you eat that tongue sand-wich?

I don't like tongue.

Why not?

I don't like the taste.

For your information, most individual food "likes" and "dislikes" are due not to any biological differences in taste cells, but to our unique personal histories of emotional and environmental food programming.

Give me an example.

If you didn't like tongue but ate it, not knowing it was tongue, you'd probably like it — but after you learned what it was and considered where it came from, your food-programmed memory bank would flash a "dislike" signal.

It all sounds very logical.

If it's logical, then why don't you eat that tongue sandwich?

I'm not hungry.

We were trapped in a heavy rainstorm.

So?

I figured, if Moses could command Nature, why couldn't I?

What did you do?

I said, "Rain, I have a secret power — after I count to ten, stop raining!"

Did it?

What do you think?

I think it kept right on raining.

Right — but I do believe it slowed down a little.

Did you ever go out people-watching?
I tried it once.
How did you like it?
It made me self-conscious.
Why?
All the people I watched were watching me.

When I lie to you, it hurts me.
Then tell the truth.
No, that's worse.
Why?
It hurts you.

People don't go to that restaurant any-more.

Why not?

It's always too crowded.

One of my phone calls could have caused a world disaster.

Clarify that.

For years I have been phoning home and asking for myself.

Weird, but no reason for disaster.

One day I phoned and I was there.

It's getting weirder.

This call — which accidentally triggered a corporeal manifestation of psychic force through a time fault molecular inversion — could have upset the natural laws of the entire universe.

How did you prevent this?

When I heard myself at the other end, I disguised my voice.

Don't take hydrogen bombs along when you go skiing,

Unless you want to make mole hills out of mountains.

I've figured out how far space goes.
How far?
To the end of time.
How long is time?
Time is endless.
Explain that more fully.
I don't have time.

Fighting with my neighbor depresses me.

Then don't fight with him.

Letting him have his own way depresses me even more.

This mosquito has a broken drill.
How does he bite people?
He doesn't.
What keeps him alive?
Transfusions.

I've decided to become well-adjusted.
Why?
So people won't notice how confused I
am.

There's one thing that can make me unhappy.

What's that?

Certain people.

What can make you happy?

Those same people.

I wonder where I'll die.
What if you knew?
I'd never go there.

Let's do something.
What, for instance?
I don't know.
There must be something to do.
I can't think of anything.
There's always one thing we can do.
What's that?
Eat.

Why are you always late?
I run out of time.
Why?
Something always comes up.
I can tell you how to be on time.
How?
Give priority to being punctual instead of to something that always comes up.

I went to another planet.
How was it?
I didn't stay.
Why not?
No place to park.

People keep telling me,
"Get on the ball."
This is ridiculous.
I know something about geography,
And I am on the ball.

When I was six, a man said to me:

"Little boy like the pretty flowers?"

I looked up from my handful of dande-lions and answered coldly:

"I have a cursory interest in botany; I was merely relating empirical criteria to the hypothesis, 'Weeds will inherit the earth'."

I never could stand condescension.

You'll have to get rid of your pet varmint.

I did already—he committed suicide.

How do you know it was suicide?

He left a note.

Let me see that note.

Can you read pet varmint?

I invented a liquid that removes all ink from paper in exactly one hour.

What have you done with this invention?

I used it to make me rich.

How?

I wrote large checks and applied the liquid.

Then what?

I cashed the checks at banks.

You mean that after one hour, the checks became pieces of blank paper?

Precisely.

Do you still cash such checks?

No.

Why not?

My parole officer won't let me.

Where did everything in the universe come from?

It was here all the time.

Before that, where was it?

Before that, there was nothing.

You mean everything came from nothing?

Look at it this way — everything has its opposite.

So?

If there is nothing, there's its opposite, which is the absence of nothing or anti-nothing.

Don't stop now.

Anti-nothing is something.

Assuming this is true, then what?

A tiny bit of anti-nothing feeds on all the nothing and grows bigger and bigger.

And is this where everything came from?

How should I know?

What's the oldest form of life?

A tortoise?

No.

An elephant?

Don't limit your answer to animal life.

A sequoia tree?

No.

What's the answer?

Bacteria — about a million years old — were discovered alive, frozen in Antarctic rocks.

I feel sorry for those bacteria.

Why?

They'll have a hard time adjusting to modern-day bacteria.

Where do fish get their food?

Basically, big fish eat small fish.

What do small fish eat?

Tiny fish.

What do tiny fish eat?

Plankton.

What's plankton?

Specks of simple plant and animal life drifting in surface waters.

What does plankton live on?

Animal plankton eats plant plankton, and plant plankton — using sunlight — makes its own food from chemicals in the water.

Is there much plankton?

Billions and billions of tons in the oceans, representing more food than is produced on the world's entire land mass.

Why can't people obtain food by extracting plankton from the sea?

It could be done, but it is more feasible to let fish do the work of extracting plankton while people, in turn, extract the fish.

Why it is more feasible?

Fish work cheaper than people.

Do you remember me?

No.

Try.

Is there any reason I should remember you?

I have an outstanding characteristic.

What is it?

I go unnoticed.

Why do you eat so much?
When I'm unhappy, food comforts me.
Why are you unhappy?
I'm socially alienated.
Why?
Why do you think?
Want a frank answer?
No, a euphemistic one.
You have a weight problem.

I'd like to escape from painful reality.
How?
By sleeping.
What stops you?
Nightmares.

How come you're so defensive?

I'm not really defensive — it's just that everyone is so offensive.

Why are you so paranoiac?

I'm not really paranoiac — it's just that everyone hates me.

He paints the horn on his head red and purple.

Whatever for?

He likes to attract attention.

I'm going to put a few moths on trial.

The charges are trespassing, willful destruction of property and having babies in my suit.

And I think, instead of pressing charges, I'm going to press moths.

You can't always trust first impressions.
Sometimes they're wrong.

For instance, I met a fellow who irritated me a little.

Later I found out differently.

He irritated me a lot.

A seed is remarkable.
Why?
It has life but it's not alive.
How do you know it's not alive?
It's not doing anything.
Well, I'm not doing anything and I'm
alive.
I'll take your word for it.

Why is he so quiet?
That girl made him self-conscious.
How did she do that?
She said, "Why are you so quiet?"

What kind of creatures did they find on that planet?

Rounds and squares.

Describe them.

Rounds are round and squares are square.

What else?

Rounds are more intelligent and rule the planet; rounds enslave squares and eat them, and make clothes out of them; some rounds make a sport of hunting and killing squares; many squares are kept in cages for display purposes.

On Earth, what corresponds to rounds?

Humans.

What corresponds to squares?

Does it surprise you when I say animals?

I once visited a penitentiary for animals.
I asked, "What's their sentence?"
"Life."
"Their crime?"
"Getting caught."
"What do you call this place?"
"Zoo."

I'm glad tomorrow's Sunday.

Why?

I'm tired of having the birds wake me at dawn.

Birds don't take Sunday off.

Oh.

That pigeon won't fly.

Why not?

He thinks flying's too dangerous.

Doesn't this handicap him?

No, fortunately this pigeon is an excellent walker.

I don't think I dream.
Everyone dreams.
It must be difficult.
On the contrary, it's simple.
Simple?
Certainly, I can do it in my sleep.

He seems more cheerful now.

Why the change?

He didn't like this world so he made up his own.

Why did you move away?
I didn't like myself in that city.
Did you improve your situation?
No, I don't like myself in this city.

How can you be certain you're not somebody else.

Because I feel like me all the time.

All the time?

Well sometimes I don't feel like myself.

Then how do you know you are yourself?

Well, it's possible I could be somebody else who's not feeling like himself.

A ghost comes here every night at exactly ten o'clock.

Nonsense.

It's true.

Ghosts don't exist.

This one does.

Parapsychologists claim that such phenomena are hallucinatory and are manifest through one's own strong need for guilt compensation or wish fulfillment.

My ghost is genuine and definitely not hallucinatory.

You're fantasizing.

Stay here until ten and you'll find out.

All right — but where are you going?

To a movie.

If he asks when you'll be back, what'll I tell him?

Today I looked in at myself and caught
myself alive.
　　I don't know what I'm doing here alive.
　　But when it comes right down to it,
　　What am I supposed to be doing?

There is no difference
Between being in love
And thinking you're in love.
The joy and pain are the same.

A little girl fell in love with a leaf.
She didn't want anyone to find her leaf,
So she hid it in a tree.

Quote poetic words to me.

"I didn't know I loved you until I saw your face in a crowd — and you weren't there."

Continue.

"No other ears but yours will hear the explosion of my soul."

More.

"Out of loneliness I will fashion a song and when I find someone who can hear my song, we will sing together."

Don't stop.

"Your mouth is a scarlet flower, bursting with honey — and I am a bee."

Delightful.

"I spread my dreams beneath your feet — tread softly."

One more.

"What I do and what I dream include you, as the wine must taste of its own grapes; and when I sue God for myself, He hears your name and sees within my eyes the tears of two."

Thank you.

What is the meaning of life?

For me — happiness.

But should you fail to find happiness, or lose it, your life would have no meaning.

Then I'd search for another meaning.

But if you searched your whole lifetime and failed, what would the meaning of life be?

The search.

I know how we'll feel after we expire.

How?

Same as before our conception — absolutely nothing.

How can you prove it?

By my cogent logic.

Can you prove it by personal experience?

I'd rather not.

Can I hold the baby chick in my hand?
Certainly.
It's so soft and small.
You're holding it too tightly.
But I love it.
You should hold what you love with an open hand.

I've decided to become happy, famous, rich, exceptionally healthy, and successful at love.

Isn't that a large order?

Well, I have to do something with my life.

Cupid shot an arrow
Into the air.
It fell to earth
And hit my typewriter
And now
This book loves you.